The Kingdom of
The Supernatural

By Ann M. Hummer
Pastor, Evangelist, and
Servant of Christ Jesus

WESTBOW
PRESS
A DIVISION OF THOMAS NELSON

WestBow Press books may be ordered through booksellers or by contacting:

WestBow Press
A Division of Thomas Nelson
1663 Liberty Drive
Bloomington, IN 47403
www.westbowpress.com
1-(866) 928-1240

Because of the dynamic nature of the Internet, any Web addresses or links contained in this book may have changed since publication and may no longer be valid. The views expressed in this work are solely those of the author and do not necessarily reflect the views of the publisher, and the publisher hereby disclaims any responsibility for them.

ISBN: 978-1-4497-0627-2 (sc)
ISBN: 978-1-4497-0628-9 (hc)
ISBN: 978-1-4497-0626-5 (e)

Library of Congress Control Number: 2010938167

Printed in the United States of America

WestBow Press rev. date: 10/19/2010

I have many Godly Men and Women I want to thank for helping me on My journey Home. I have heard each speak several times and some of them, most, are on TV.

Pastor John Hagee- jhm.org
Sid Roth, It's Supernatural- sidroth.org
Charles and Joan Hunter- cfhunter.org
John Ankerburg- jashow.org
Dr. Jimmy DeYoung
Drs. Jack and Rexella Van Impe- jvim.com
Dr. David Reagan- lamblion.com
Perry Stone, Manna Fest- perrystone.org
Chuck Missler-on the God channel
Rabbi Yechiel Eckstein-International Fellowship of Christians and Jews- ifcj.org

A little food for thought:

Every seed produces it's own-
Sow apple seeds, and you get apples
Sow a smile, and you will get one
Sow kindness, and you will get kindness

Here are some of my favorite scriptures:

This is the day the Lord has made; Let us rejoice and be glad in it.
- Psalm 118 verse 24

We love because He first loved us
- 1 John verse19

Anyone who speaks against His brother or judges him, speaks against the law and judges it.
- James 4 verse 11

We are a mist that appears for a little while and then vanishes
- James 4 verse 14

All scripture is given by the inspiration of God
- 2 Timothy verse 16

My grace is sufficient for you, for my power is made perfect in weakness
- 2 Corinthians 12 verse 9

If I were still trying to please Man, I would not be a servant of Christ
- Galatians 1 verse 10

I have been crucified with Christ and I no longer live, but Christ lives in Me
- Galatians 2 verse 20

The only thing that counts is faith expressing itself through Love
- Galatians 5 verse 6

I can do anything through Him who gives me strength
- Philippians 4 verse 13

He sent His word and Healed them
- Psalm 107 verse 20

Greater is He that's in Me, than he that's in the world
- 1 John 4 verse 4

Weeping may endure for a night, but Joy comes in the morning
- Psalm 30 verse 5

Those that sow in tears, shall reap in Joy
- Psalm 126 verse 5

Enter into the joy of your Lord
- Matthew 25 verse 21

I have no greater joy than to hear that my children walk in truth
- 3 John 1 verse 4

But seek first the kingdom of God and His righteousness, and all these thing shall be added to you
-Matthew 6 verse 33

Give, and it will be given to you: good measure, pressed down, shaken together, and running over will be put in your bosom. For with the same measure you use, it will be measured back to you
- Luke 6 verse 38

And my God shall supply all your needs according to His riches in glory by Christ Jesus
- Philippians 4 verse 19

The curse of the Lord is on the house of the wicked, but He blesses the home of the just
- Proverbs 3 verse 33

The Lord is my shepherd, I shall not want
- Psalm 23

No weapon formed against you shall prosper
- Isaiah 54 verse 17

Who Himself bore our sins in His own body
on a tree, that we, having died to sins, might
live for righteousness, by whose stripes you were
healed
-1 Peter verse 24

A merry heart does good, like medicine, but a
broken spirit dries the bones
- Proverbs 17 verse 22

I have heard your prayer, I have seen your tears;
surely I will heal you
- 2 kings 20 verse 5

Behold, I am the Lord, the God of all flesh. Is
there anything too hard for Me?
- Jeremiah 32 verse 27

He heals the brokenhearted and binds up
their wounds
- Psalm 147 verse 3

Jesus, the same yesterday, today, and forever
- Hebrews 13 verse 8

Resist the devil and he must flee
- James 4 verse 7

He called things into being, that are not
- Romans 4 verse 17

Are not all angels ministering spirits sent to serve those who will inherit salvation?
- Hebrews 1 verse 14

I SHALL NOT DIE, BUT LIVE, AND DECLARE THE WORKS OF THE LORD!
- Psalm 118 verse 17

Remember---

If you are rejected, you are NOT defeated! God is with you!

God is NOT mad! He loves you very much.

As a man thinkest, he is! SO be Positive, act like a winner, and you will be!

Even satan believes in God.

But the fruit of the spirit is Love, Joy, Peace, patience, kindness, goodness, faithfulness, Gentleness, and Self- Control---Galatians 5 verse 22

I dedicate this Book to:

My Lord and Savior Jesus Christ

My Husband Kenneth

My Children, Kimberly, Ken, and Angela

My Grandkids and Greatest Joys:

Nikolas, Ashtyn, Noah, Isaiah,
Paolo, Gracie, and Matthew

My Sister, Trisha, and the joy of her life, Her
Granddaughter, Claire

My two best Friends- Bobbie and Joanie
My friend - Cliff
My cousin - Donna
To all my friends I just haven't met yet!

What do you think of when you hear the word

SUPERNATURAL?

Maybe the occult, devil worshipers, ooo a graveyard, witchcraft, how about terra-cards, maybe Halloween, how about Hell Itself. You know, these are of satan and he doesn't even come close to my Supernatural. Well maybe not a graveyard, as this is just a resting place for our Loved ones and us until our Loving Savior calls us home when He comes for us at The Rapture. How glorious it would be if I'm setting at my Mother and Fathers' grave when He calls. As the dead in Christ will rise first, then we that remain will be called up to meet Him in the clouds! To God Be The Glory! Go to verse 1st Thessalonians chapter 4 verses 16-18.

When I think of the supernatural, I think of Peace, beyond all understanding, Love, the kind

1

that overtakes your whole being, and Life Eternal in a place called Heaven! That's what I have been promised, and you can have all this, too!

Which of these sound like the best Supernatural to you? Eternal Life that our Father has planned for us or eternal damnation that satan has planned for us? Do you know that the choice is YOURS and that you can be assured that you will wind up in one of these!

It's a no-brainer for me! I have heard people say that Heaven is going to be boring, praising God 24/7. What a misconception!! God made man to interact with Him, to be His companion on this Earth. He gave us

everything we needed to flourish and evolve, including a mate to Love and be our companion. Then, Sin came into being because of mans'(and womans') temptation with Satan. Most of you know that story, but for the ones that don't, go to your Bible and read Genesis chapter 3 verse 1-19 of the NIV Bible.

He made us in His Image! How cool is that! Genesis 1 verse 27. Since then, we have a Sin

Nature, born in sin and yet God still loves us and wishes no one to be lost (lose our salvation).

He sent His only Son, born of a Virgin, Mary, to die a horrible death on a cross to atone (or erase) our sin with His Precious Blood. Could you even imagine sacrificing your child that you Love so much? I know I couldn't! How much more Love could He have for US! There is a story in the Bible of a man named Abraham that loved and trusted God so much, that when God tested his love by telling him to sacrifice his beloved son Isaac, he was so saddened but set out to do Gods' will. God stopped Abraham from completing this act to show Him how much Love He had for Him. You can read this story in Genesis chapter 22 verse 1-14. What a great God we serve.

We have only touched the surface of God's love for us, read John 14, what a loving Father we have! I went to see the movie " The Passion of Christ . It really brought this story of God's love to life. I saw the pain and suffering of our Lord Jesus and was overcome with grief. Even though this was a movie, I couldn't even see this movie for a second time, You see, this IS a true story. His precious Mother, Mary, was there watching

His crucifixion, My heart can't even imagine the torment She and Her family and friends were going through. They nailed his hands to the cross, pierced His side, and mocked Him as He was dying on this cross. In severe pain and almost unconscious, He still had compassion for His killers as He said, ' Forgive them Father, as they know not what they do". What kind of Love could this possibly be? Thank God we have a Savior like this! Luke 23, chapter 26-49.

Now for the Good News, He was placed in a cave-type grave with a Huge stone to keep Him in and to keep others out. BUT, no grave could keep Him! He died on Friday, rested on the Sabbath, and rose from His grave on Sunday. Continue reading Luke 23 chapter 50-chapter 24 verse 12. These verses I'm giving you are from the NIV Holy Bible. He died a devastating death, for What? For You and Me, so our sins could be forgiven and His blood be our atonement of sin. When you hear, we are washed in His Blood, this is what that means. HOW could SO many stay away from a loving Savior like this? I can only believe maybe it's the fear of the unknown. The fear of the Supernatural? As God is a spirit. Or maybe you know you have things in your life that He would NOT approve of. For me, it was a fear of God, I couldn't understand what I tried to read in the Bible, I must Not be of Gods family! I now know that Satan was messing with my head. He kept my mind so full of stuff from Life that I couldn't keep the JUNK out of my head long enough to concentrate on anything I would read, especially the Bible! I must have made satan so proud! Just get in YOUR secret place , with your Bible and say a little prayer before you start reading. Just something as simple as "Father God, Please clear my mind as I read your words and let me enter your kingdom, In Jesus Name, Amen. You may ask why " In Jesus Name"? You see, Jesus is our intercessor! He carries our prayers to our Heavenly Father. Everything we ask goes through Jesus. You see, He is the ONLY way to our Heavenly Father. Read Acts 4 verse 12. Well, God Loves you and there is nothing He won't forgive you for, well except for one, and that's blaspheming of the Holy Spirit. What's the Holy Spirit, you asked? Good Question! You see, it was only about thirteen years ago when I started to understand what or who this is. I never heard of this in any church or sermon I had heard. However, this is one of the most important things you will ever need to understand. If I had known of this many years ago, I could have had a much greater life and would have had a much greater impact on others. I could have had The Peace, His Perfect peace I know today, even with all the trails I have suffered in this life. As I continue, I pray that EVERYONE will at some point of their Life, know the Peace of MY FATHER. The Holy Spirit, the third of the trinity, " The Father, the Son, and The Holy Spirit". God has promised the Holy Spirit to all who Love Him.

We have a spirit breathed in us by God at birth, called the breath of life, but a greater Spirit will overcome us when we accept Him and HIS COMMANDMENTS. Some of us know that there is ten of these. We are to follow all, as these are of God, not man. No. 1 you shall have no other Gods besides Him, No. 2, You shall make no idols of anything to worship. I believe this includes our homes, our money, our cars and trucks, or any other adult toys we may own. They were put on this Earth for our enjoyment, not to worship. We are to worship God, our Savior, alone! These things will not make it to Heaven with us anyway! But don't dismay, as our Father has many greater things in store for us when we get there. No. 3, You shall never take the Lord's name in vane or misuse it in anyway, for you will not be held guiltless. Repent of this and you can be forgiven. No. 4, Remember the Sabbath and keep it Holy. God said we are to work six days and on the seventh day we are to rest, as He did. The Lord blessed the Sabbath and made it Holy. This really bothers me as most of us have always used Sunday as the Sabbath. Have we been mislead, as the seventh day is Saturday. The Holy Spirit has laid this heavily on my mind and in my heart. You see, the days of the week have never changed sense time began, although calendars have. No. 5, Honor your father and mother, this one comes with a special gift from God that you may have a long life in the land your Lord has given you. No. 6, You shall not murder. No. 7, You shall not commit adultery. No. 8, You shall not steal. No. 9, You shall not lie. God detests a liar, so watch what comes out of your mouth! No. 10, You shall not covet anything that your neighbor has. We are to follow His Commandments, Exodus chapter 20 verse 1 through 17, and His Laws, which are all throughout the New Testament. If you read this and know you have already been condemned, I have great news, just go to your Heavenly Father in prayer and ask Him to come into your heart and save you and forgive you of your sins and He promises to forgive you and make you a new person! To God Be The Glory! This is just what I did.

I have asked God to anoint every word in this book to His Glory, not mine as I am nothing without Him. BUT, with Him there is no stopping Me now! He told me to write this book so I know it is already anointed and blessed.

I get so exited when I feel the Holy Spirit come upon me. This usually happens to me when I'm reading His Word, The Bible, as He Tells us He is the WORD, also The Way, The Truth, and The Life. Sometimes, when I'm reading my Bible, I feel as if He is reading it to me. This really puts me in a great state of peace. I feel the presence of the Holy Spirit when I get caught up in my singing of His songs(as I feel myself getting louder and louder), as if it's just Me and Him in the room. It's been said that when you are singing, you are praising Him twice! If you have ever sit in front of me at Church, I apologize for my loudness but not for the Holy Spirit that caused it! I feel the Holy Spirit come upon me as I pray for people individually, it is so awesome!

Sometimes I hear words coming out of my mouth that are not mine, and I praise Him for that as He knows what people need to hear better than I do. I have felt the Holy Spirit many many times as you will hear in my testimonies to come. Just let me start talking of our Savior and He just takes over My being! I have a good friend that will call me from Myrtle Beach and ask me things about the Bible and sometimes the Holy Spirit fills me with a whole Sermon and we are on the phone for hours!

I grew up in a little town in northern Virginia, Lovettsville. Our little town borders Maryland and West Virginia. I left there in the 80's with my family. My parents owned a grocery store there, so we knew just about everyone that lived in the town.

What a different time that was! No one locked their doors, there was no violence, no drugs, it was a time of freedom and peace. We always woke up on Saturdays and Sundays to other people that had spent the night with one of us. As I said, doors always open! Thinking back, what a different time as we lock every door in the house now and have to have elaborate security systems! Will we ever feel secure again?

I remember one of my very favorite things to do was to sit on our big front porch when it was raining and eat popsicles with my Dad and siblings and wave to the neighbors as they drove by. Mom was always working in the store to make sure we always had those popsicles. It was a simple life, we never went out unless it was to my Grandmas, Dad's Mom, for dinner some Sundays.

There was never a threat to anyone, no drugs, only the occasional moonshine or hard cider that my brothers would partake. I laugh at remembering them at a young age, maybe about 11 to 13, staggering up the back street, with a friend after being in my Uncle's barn. That was a sight to behold! It's funny how some little things in life stand out and bring a chuckle to mind! I recently went to my Uncle's nursing home, the one that owned that farm at that time, and told him about this memory. It was great to reminisce with Him and we both had a great laugh as he had never heard this story before.

When I was just six years old, I had rheumatic fever, I didn't know it then but I was really sick. My Dad would have to carry me to the bathroom and back for six weeks. I received tons of cards everyday from the people in our town and I would get a shot of penicillin everyday from our local Doc. My siblings were always around me keeping me company. I know now that God had a plan for my life and I recovered to His Glory!

I remember my favorite story back then was " The Little Match Girl'. I may be telling my age now, but I think I identified with her on so many levels, torn dresses, dirty faces, skinny, and just pitiful, or maybe I just loved her and felt so sorry for her. I know I have so much Love in me. I love so much deeper than others I know. I trusted everyone and believed what anyone said. I guess I was a little naïve, also. I remember when my oldest brother made some kool-aid and told me to have some. Being so gullible, I remember spitting and gagging and chocking as it was rabbit blood and water! That sure made his day! I think I became less naïve that day!

Our family needs were always met. Having a grocery store, at least we never went hungry and our basic needs were met. We didn't get much through the year, but when it came to Birthdays and especially Christmas, they were my greatest memories. I continued those holidays as I remembered home, for my children and then my grandchildren. I loved every minute of their excitement. It's like going home again once a year. We always had a cake that said "Happy Birthday Jesus," keeping the real meaning of Christmas at hand and celebrating with loved ones.

As a young child, I remember our babysitter, she wasn't too educated as I recall. My punishment was to be locked in that dark closet under the staircase. I still can remember the stench of moth balls as Dad's war uniforms were stored in there. In my adult life, I have always hated the dark, wonder why? I'm sure my parents had no knowledge of this.

My Dad was in WW2, the second wave at Normandy Beach, France. He picked up bodies and wounded soldiers off the beach, as the first wave had been ambushed.

My Dad, I realized as I became an adult, had such anxiety from this war. As I carry much anxiety of His in my own life. You see, I was Dad's pet . I've been told that he took care of me as an infant as he had a heart attack before I was born. So I laid on the bed beside him so Mom could continue working in the store. Being born on Veteran's Day, November 11, was also a feather in my cap! As I know now, Dad would have panic attacks, back then we would just call them nerve spells.

Dad would get out his gun and would start sweating profusely. I never knew who his target would be, but somehow my little brain would know it wasn't me. I was smart enough to know that you don't kill the ones you love, at least that was my analogy at my tender age of five. I was the one that had to talk him out of hurting anyone. I remember crying, " Daddy, I love you, Daddy, I love you, over and over and over again until he would put the gun down. This happened more than once, but I have forgiven Him many times over as I knew it was something to do with the war. I always knew I wouldn't be killed as I Loved Him so much. I just knew He wasn't mad at me, as I always tried to think of ways to please Him. I remember my dear Sister, Carolyn, who died of cancer much too soon, and I would get a bucket of water and soap and wash his feet as they hung out from the end of the bed. He loved this and we did it often. I just knew this was enough to keep us from being shot, because in my young thinking, he wouldn't get His feet washed anymore!

Wow, I haven't thought of these things in so many years and my emotions right now are really feeling sorry for this little girl I am remembering. I wasn't afraid, but always hoping Dad's attacks would not come back again. This was just my life, as I assumed every daddy had a gun!!

Then came the growing up part. Falling in love, having three beautiful kids. My first daughter was so beautiful, her skin was like an angel, I can't even describe it as her face looked like a heavenly cream. I have never seen another child's skin that angelic. Next I had my Son, the most handsome baby boy I have ever seen, His little face was so pretty but he still looked masculine. As he grew, a total little stinker emerged and so much Fun. He was always playing pranks on everybody and blaming them on His cousin. Then came my youngest daughter, a real cutie-pie. She clung to me like a teddy bear. If she saw a picture of herself alone, she would cry "Where's Her Mom-my?" So precious! She was my little Prima-Ballerina. I had so much fun raising my children, in many respects, I grew up with them. I tell you the truth, they were never going to see the childhood I had lived through. I now knew what love was all about as they clung to me for everything, and I clung right back to them vowing to never let them go. Then came the GRANDKIDS!

I believe that grand kids are truly the greatest rewards that we can have in our older lives. I have enjoyed each one in many different ways as they each are so different, but their Love for me is so sincere. As long as I have my grandchildren, I know I am Loved!

Enough about me right now, as I have had amazing things happen in my life. Things that still make me in awe of our Lord and Savior, Jesus Christ. And I still wonder: HOW could He Love ME so much! I now know He chose me to show compassion in this world, as I have always had a heart of giving, not caring if I ever received anything or not. In fact , I'm not a very good receiver, it does't feel right to me when someone gives me things, as I know that I never give things in order to receive them. It's hard to explain, but I just want to give as the feeling I get is such a euphoric sense. I guess you could say ' A Natural High'. Through the years I remember always helping people at Christmas that didn't have gifts for their families or just down on their luck for a while, just needing to know someone cared. I always helped with food but God gave me a heart for the children. When you give something to a child that hasn't had much and look into their precious faces, you are really blessing their parents. When I can do this it is like the biggest blessing ever, to get a hug and a thank-you from a Mom with tears streaming down her face. This is the Heart that God gave Me and He gets all the praise and glory in everything I can do to further HIS Kingdom. I challenge everyone of you to find a family to help in their time of need. Right now with the economy the way it is, this won't be a challenge to find a family that could use just some kindness and a little help. You will get the Blessing, I guarantee it! The Bible says to Love your neighbor as yourself.

As I write about my tests in this life, you remember some of your tests, and see if you can turn them into a TESTIMONY!

I must begin my testimonies by telling you that I had always been a good person, so in my eyes I didn't really need to go to church very often, I felt I had the basics of Christianity and I had allowed my work to take over my being. Let me say right now, that was the BIGGEST Mistake of my Life! And it will be the Biggest mistake of your life, too especially if you have children. If you don't raise them in Church you are not giving them the foundation they deserve. I can speak by experience! And I agonize over this. My biggest mistake in Life! (This is worth repeating). I apologize to all three of My children for this, as it is hard for them to understand why this bothers me so much. How can they think God is so important. I pray every night that God will give them wisdom in this area! Many people in these times think that God is not that important, When in fact , He is the ONLY thing that is important!

I was very competitive at work and felt I could do anything, I enjoyed competing in a Man's World. I came from a family that had a grocery store and my mother taught me to cut meat. That gave me the courage to find work in a grocery chain. There I began my career. I worked diligently in the meat department, as my kids were almost grown by then and I knew I was needed less and less at home, as I had taught the kids how to cook and clean. My Mom was so proud of all my promotions I was getting, since she taught me to cut meat, however I still had to go through a two year training program. Then, I just kept competing in every way I could. I went from meat cutter, to first cutter, to meat manager, with the encouragement of a certain meat supervisor, I went to the gourmet Meat departments, learning all those gourmet cuts was my forte. From there, I became a gourmet meat specialist, a trainer, and then a Gourmet Meat Supervisor and had 158 gourmet meat departments under my supervision. George, thanks for being the wind beneath my wings! That was a great time in my corporate life! Even though that was a great time in my life and I was having the time of my life, that was still not even close to the Life that God had and has planned for the rest of my life. But this shows how ONE person can have a profound influence on another persons life. Again, find someone you can help and they will not forget your help, maybe they will pass it on and be a help to others. A snowball effect would be a great legacy to have.

In the mid 90's I came down with a debilitating and painful illness called fibromyalgia and chronic fatigue. My corporate days were over.

In '96 my knee went out and I had to have surgery. I literally left work hardly able to walk to my car.

I was resting on my bed after having surgery in the middle of the day, just starring at my little round stained glass angel plaque hanging from my light in the center of my bedroom, a gift from a close friend, Bobbie.

When suddenly I heard a voice and a shock went through my whole being! This was my first real encounter with the Lord. God spoke to me that day and changed my life Forever!

As I was hearing(not with my ears but in my mind but I was totally entranced and realized I couldn't turn my thoughts). The words He spoke to me were " I Will Always Be With You, You Will Never Be Alone." This was repeated to me at least 20 times over and over again. Softly at first, and then got louder and louder, then back to soft. As these words were spoken to me, that stained glass angel started moving in the same manner as the voice I was hearing. Small movement at first , then as the voice got louder the angel moved faster then back to softly again. It moved to the tone of the voice and when the voice stopped so did the movement of the angel. I remember just laying there wondering what just happened! I was able to change my thoughts again. It was so peaceful, a peace I had never felt before and I noticed I was smiling. My first thought was "Am I losing my mind or did I have a real encounter with God?" "WOW," I thought, "God really knows Me!" What an epiphany I Had! This was awesome. I wanted to scream it to the Top of My Lungs! Then reality set in and I knew everyone would think I was Nuts! You see, most people couldn't believe something like this, it's just too far out there and I was having trouble believing it myself, but of course I did!

I just knew after this experience, God had something planned for my life, but little did I know the magnitude of what was to come.

To God Be The Glory! I give God all the praise and glory for the experiences He gives me! And when things get tough I remember Him saying to me " I'll always be with you , you'll never be alone." It gets me through every time as you will see as you continue reading. I pray that everyone that this testimony reaches be blessed and know too, that each one of you have a personal Savior, Jesus Christ.

I could hardly wait now to see how God was going to use me. One Sunday, in early April, 1997 a strange feeling came over me, I understand now that it was The Holy Spirit, I heard that voice in my mind again. It said "Find Penny, Find Penny," It had a sense of urgency about it, A chill came over me! Penny was a good friend of mine in years past, about 18 years earlier. We had bowled on the same team back then, that's where we first met. We had a great year and became good friends. We took our families on picnics together and we went fishing and swimming in Her fathers pond. We won trophies at our bowling banquets. Life was good! She was the sweetest person I knew and she really loved my kids. Then after bowling , we kind of went our separate ways. I took my job in a grocery chain and she went to work also. We would only see each other briefly at the mall or grocery shopping, but we always took a few minutes to sit awhile and catch up with what each of our families were doing. I know now that God had already set His plan for me many years ago!

So now let's get back to that feeling I had on that Sunday in April' 97. It was like nothing I had ever experienced before. I knew I Had to find Penny, I just knew in my being she needed me somehow.

At this time my Mother was living in Lovettsville, Virginia with my sister Trisha. The next day I went to see Mom and out of the blue, My sister asked me if I had heard that Penny was in a nursing home dying of cancer. I was so shocked at this, I could barely catch my breath!

You can only imagine the chills that went up my spine! I knew this is where I had been called. You know if I hadn't had that visitation from God the day before, I might have done nothing more than send her a card. There is no way I could have handled going to see a friend dying, especially Penny, on my own.

I knew she was in a Leesburg, Virginia nursing home, but where was I going to start looking as this town had many nursing homes. But not to my surprise, she was at the first place I called. When God calls you for his glory, He will make it easy when you say, yes, Lord, I'll go!

However, I was so afraid to talk to her as I wasn't good at being around sick people. I was a meat cutter by trade, but I couldn't stomach human blood, as it made me very nauseous. I had lost a sister, Carolyn, to cancer in 1987 and didn't know how to help her very well. I was so distraught, it was hard to know how to comfort her. I did my best though, not knowing God as I do today. I have to say though, God had rallied a ton of her best friends around her as they were all willing to help her. I thank God for each and everyone of them. I hope they read this book someday, as I want to thank each of them, thank you Jean, Joyce, Karen, as they stayed nights along with my sisters, Mom, and me. We all took turns spending the nights so Carolyn wouldn't be alone. If I missed anyone, I thank you all.

Now back to Penny, I was scared out of my wits, but I silently prayed and asked God to give me the right words to say. I remember our conversation quite vividly, I guess I'll never forget it. I made the call and asked for Penny's room.

"Penny," I said, Yes, she replied. "This is Ann, do you feel like having company?" She broke down crying, "Ann, please come, please come".

I told her I would be there soon. I thought to myself "But what good could I possibly be to her as I was sick, in pain, and had such fatigue! But I knew I had to go.

As I was driving to the nursing home, I guess I got a little nervous as I begin to argue with God about His decision to send me, I told Him that I wasn't the one for this job as I don't know what to say or do that could possibly help Penny in any way! As now, I was yelling and screaming and telling God how scared I was. It was a wonder God didn't strike me down with my "I can't do this" attitude. Then all of a sudden a peace came over me and I just asked for Him to help me and give me strength to comfort her. When I pulled up to the nursing home, I put my head down on the steering wheel for a minute. Then I finally said, God, your will be done, not mine." I honestly believe that moment I was filled with The Holy Spirit as when My head raised I felt I could do Anything!

As I went into her room, the tears welled up in her eyes as I ran up and hugged her. I was determined not to cry as she needed me to be strong. I remember going into a numb state as if God had his arms around us both.

As we talked I heard a bitterness in her voice, she started crying and shouting, " Why did God do this to me, I don't want anything to do with Him, what did I do to deserve this? She was so angry with God, and she had already been through so much. Her husband, Billy, had drowned on a fishing trip several years earlier, in the Agnes Flood because he couldn't swim. She just lost her fiancée, that died just a week earlier across the hall in this same nursing home of cancer. How do you console someone that had all this happen to them and was now dying herself. However, it was not my place to question. My purpose was to help her anyway I could. I knew God wouldn't leave me, as He had told me earlier that He would never leave me, He would always be with me, and He ministered to her through me. I remember my first conversation with her was " Penny, God didn't do this to you, He only wants what is best for His children." She interrupted saying, " Then why doesn't He make me well?" Boy, I knew now this was going to get tough. I told Penny God could make her well if it is His will and that we would pray for her recovery, but she needed to understand that ultimately God's will be done. I reminded her that Satan is running rampant in this world, and to look at what we humans have done to the environment: all the toxins, smoke, and factory smog polluting our world. God hadn't intended for us to destroy the earth as we have. This was satan, not God. I told her that God loved her, and now I knew why He sent me.

I had such little time to make her understand. I knew He would not take her until she knew the truth about Him. I knew now, She would not enter the gates of heaven until she changed her attitude about Him. See the lengths your heavenly Father will go to for your salvation. I consider myself just a regular person, but in God's eyes, He saw me as mighty and chose Me to bring Penny back to His kingdom! This is the ultimate reward I could possibly Have been given. To bring a child of God, back to Him. The Bible says that God will use the lowest to be the greatest! I do not feel adequate but very humble that I could serve our Mighty God in this way. What a journey I am on at this point.

I had stayed several hours with her, and I remember what she said to me, " Ann, I know you have a family to go home to, but could you stay a little longer?" I told her "I'll be with you for as long as you need me." I stayed each day with her, reading her devotionals, talking to her about our loving God, and just trying to be her friend. I wasn't able to spend the nights, but the nursing home allowed me to stay 9 am to 9 pm. That was the rules of the facility. I drove over an hour twice a day to be with her. Penny had a roommate, Mrs. Anderson. She told me she had tried to console Penny but to no avail. I would pull up my chair between them and read, play tapes, and sing hymns. I remember one day, I was caught up in my singing when Penny asked me to stop. I was praising my Savior, and she was sick of my singing. I remember bursting out laughing as that was the first time I had been told to shut up singing before, but remembering that I could get carried away when I sing to my Lord! But just then as I was laughing, Penny burst out laughing, too. It was probably the biggest laugh we had ever had together. Every night before I left for home, Penny, Mrs. Anderson, and I would have prayer. Then Penny would always ask me if I was coming back tomorrow, even though I always did. She just needed each night to hear me say it.

After about three weeks, Mrs. Anderson passed away, what a dear lady she was. How strange it was, I didn't know until the night she was dying(when her family came in) that I had gone to school with her son. I felt so blessed as her family told me what a blessing I had been to her. I didn't realize how I, with God's help, had been a blessing to Mrs. Anderson, but she had told her family of me. I was truly humbled.

Earlier, Mrs. Anderson had told me that she had cheated death six times but that she was at peace now. She thanked me over and over again. You can't imagine how this made me feel.

I went to Mrs. Anderson's viewing and as I entered the door, everyone just turned around and greeted me with " There's Penny's Angel!" I did feel a little angelical at that moment, but also a little embarrassed or maybe just humbled, I guess. I do give God all the Glory for using me to help Mrs. Anderson.

As I went to the nursing home one morning, about three or four nurses ran to meet me. They didn't want me to see Penny's empty bed, as she had been admitted to the hospital. She had lung cancer and her lungs were filling up and she had to have a chest tube to drain them. But there was even a blessing for Penny in this move. I also need to say that the nurses Penny had were just great, not only to her but me, also.

When I got to the hospital, Penny seemed so elated as she said " Ann, Now you can stay with me and spend the nights, too." God bless her, she was seeing the good in everything now! I remember I burst out laughing and told her I was getting tired of driving home anyway!

Then they brought Penny her meal menu, she wasn't eating a lot these days, but she started marking lots of things on this card. I said "Are you getting your apatite back?" She said " No, I'm marking this for you so you won't have to leave to go eat." As she didn't allow me to leave her room. So, we both just ate off her tray, I do remember I lost a good bit of weight while there, but that was a blessing to me!

That night, now you need to remember my chronic fatigue, I pulled up a terribly uncomfortable broken recliner. The leg part would not go up, so I pulled it out the best I could, a nurse gave me a blanket and a pillow, and set it right beside her bed. We held hands all night long. To God's Glory, I slept all night that night even though I hardly could sleep at home due to my fibromyalgia. It marvels me to realize that I slept like a baby every night, holding hands with my friend. I knew she was in so much agony and pain but she would try not to wake me as she was afraid if I didn't get enough rest I would have to leave because of my illness. She had become so dependant on me and I knew she was getting weaker and weaker all the time. I knew I just had to see it through. I remember one time when she got so critical, I didn't leave her room, not even to shower or change for four days because of two promises I had made to her. She had made me promise that I would be with her when she died, and also to help her son if he needed me. I had been through a lot but, with God's help,

The Holy Spirit, and my love for Penny, I knew I would have the strength.

I remember one day getting ridiculed once in the hospital. A so-called friend of Penny's, in fact I knew her too as she had bowled with us years ago, caught me in the hall of the hospital and asked me why I was doing this for Penny as she said that Penny wouldn't do this for me. She kind of hit me off guard, as that had never come into my thoughts. I just looked at her and said, " I would do it for you." Needless to say, she just walked away.

I also remember that someone in the hospital, I believe it to be a nurse I knew, called my daughter to come get me and take me home. I remember my daughter, with tears flowing down her face, and her husband, trying to get me to leave. Well, that wasn't going to happen in this lifetime! However, I told them I would go home, take a shower, get something to eat(I'm not complaining about the hospital food) only if they would stay with My Penny until I got back, as she was not going to be alone for one minute if I could help it,

That's what I did! My Father in Heaven had given me charge over Penny and I took it Very seriously.

One night, around midnight, I woke up. Penny was starring at the ceiling, our hands were still clutched in each others'. I just knew at that time it couldn't be much longer.

Softly I asked her, Penny, what do you see?" She said in a saddened voice " Ann's crying, I see Ann crying." I felt this was nearing the end, but being human, and very numb now, I wanted to know all she was seeing. I asked her very softly, " Penny, why am I crying?" She said she didn't know. I asked her to look around and let me know what she was seeing. She waited a few seconds and said, "I see a light." I asked her if she could go toward the light and she said yes. I was speaking so low as I wanted her to go now and be out of that horrible pain she was in. Seconds went by and I asked her again, " are you still going toward the light?" She replied again in a very soft voice, " yes." I asked her what she was seeing now, as her eyes had stayed fixed on the ceiling. She was quiet for about two or three minutes. Then she yelled out in her weakened state, "I see Jesus, I see Jesus!" I said, "can you go with Jesus?" she said "yes, I'm going with Jesus." By now I'm getting so emotional and was feeling tears welling up in me. This was the crying she had been seeing me do. But, we were on a journey now and I asked her if she could see an Angel. She kind of seemed agitated for a moment then said "Yes, but it's too many, I can't count them." I immediately said, " No Honey, you don't have to count them, just go with them. She replied faintly, " okay, I'm going. I had decided not to ask anything more as this was her journey and I did not want anything I might say to interrupt. I just sit there holding her hand. I felt if she wanted to say more or if for some reason, THEY wouldn't want her to tell me more, I had already been Blessed for a lifetime with the knowledge she had already given me. A few minutes went by and Penny, speaking in a childlike voice said, " I see Daddy! I see Daddy!, Daddy wants me to come play." I told her to go to Daddy, go play with Daddy. Then she said almost crying "awe, Mommy, Mommy, I see Mommy!" I remember that Penny's Mom had died when she was very young, I think she had told me when she was around nine, but her Daddy had not been dead too long as I had seen him several times. I said to Penny, "Go to Mommy and Daddy."

I was expecting her to let go and pass, but what came next Almost Scared Me To Death!

Penny started screaming " NO! NO! NO! If Ann can't come I don't want to come. " Ann, they said it's not your time yet, but I'm not going if you can't go. She screamed, " Please Let Ann Go, Too."

At this point, I started hyperventilating; I could hardly catch my breath, my life did flash before me, all I could think of was my Children and my Grandchildren! To my shock, and that's putting it lightly, I said, "Penny! I'll come later, you go with Mommy and Daddy, and I'll come later." She said, " NO, If Ann can't go I'm not going!" By this time she was screaming. I tried to calm her down and let her know she would be out of pain and in Glory but by this time she was hysterical. I felt so bad and even a bit guilty that she had become so attached to me and wouldn't leave me even though her pain and suffering was tremendous. I asked her to calm down and focus on Heaven. I asked her to look around and see if she could see the light. She looked up and said, " It's only the sun." That was the last words she said to me, as she then went into a coma-like state but I continued to be with her and talk to her about heaven and God's love that could take her out of pain. She wasn't entirely comatose as she still would feel pain and moan, but was unable to speak to me anymore.

I had seen heaven that night through the eyes of Penny. What a gift I had been given by God!

The following Sunday morning around eight o'clock, Penny started throwing up a lot of blood clots. My first reaction was to call the nurses, then I just reacted! I have found that The Holy Spirit will cause you to react and sometimes give you no time to think! So, I ran to the other side of the bed and put my fingers down her throat and began to clear her airways. I had watched a nurse do this before so I felt confident in what I was doing. Plus I had my Lord with me, what else did I need, and no way was I going to let her die like that. I knew if I had waited on the nurse, I would have seen her die a horrible death. If I had anything to do with it, she was at least going to die in peace. At this time, a friend of Pennys' came in and saw what was happening and asked if her family had been called, by this time the nurse was there helping me, but I told Penny's friend to make the call as we had been too busy to do it yet. I remember the dear nurse helping me with tears in her eyes as though she was reading my very thoughts. She told me, "If only I could have someone like you with me when my time is up." That was so sweet!

I just couldn't bear to have her choke to death, I wanted her to be able to go in peace, that was my prayer. Miraculously, the bleeding stopped as if God himself was answering my prayer right then! Her family all came and stayed for hours until she was stable again. Penny didn't have much family left on this earth, only a cousin, mother in law, father in law and her son, but Penny had a multitude of loving friends that surrounded her. Penny's Pastor came often and always called me Penny's Angel. I'm not sure He even knew my name.

To know Penny was to love Penny. Her son and his girlfriend came on that Sunday, even though he had quit coming to see her for weeks. She would call him and leave messages on his answering machine and literally beg him to come see her, but he would make excuses and promises to come, even though he didn't show up. I knew he just couldn't bear to see her so sick, but now he was here and God was in charge! God was getting ready to work through me again! As Penny was stabilizing again and family began to leave, I asked him if he would come back that evening and he did around seven o'clock. His Mom didn't open her eyes at all after this episode of bleeding.

Now I realized God was back in action as I turned to him, with his head leaned over resting in his hands and looking so disturbed and sitting as far away from his mother as he could. Quietly, I asked God for the right words to help him. Then out of my mouth came, What do you need? How can I help you? A couple of minutes of silence went by and then he looked up at me and said, "Is there a Heaven? I said with sympathy and enthusiasm, " Oh yes, there is a heaven and it's so glorious. There is no more sickness, no grief or pain, only love and fellowship and praising God." Then he asked, " What will happen to Mom when she dies?" I explained my faith and beliefs that at the moment of death her spirit, which is her " real" being, would be lifted up from her body and she will be with Jesus and united with her loved ones in heaven. Then I began telling him about her near death experience that night with me. Bless His heart, he started throwing one question after another at me about Jesus, God, Heaven. And hell(you will notice that in my book hell and satan never get a capital letter!) I just opened my mouth and God poured out the answers. He began getting comfortable with me and my answers until his voice was no longer trembling. He was smiling, laughing, and started telling me stories about his Mom and the animals she had named on the farm she had lived on. I had witnessed another miracle! In no time, he was sitting by his Mom's bed and touching her and talking to her, I just knew that somehow she was hearing him.

Before we knew it, it was 2am. He had been there from 7pm till 2am. To God be the Glory! It was a miracle come true. He came back every night until her passing on that Thursday. I had seen and been part of another blessing!

During those six weeks I had been with Penny, I had been blessed enough for a lifetime! God had me doing and saying things that I would never have thought I could do or say!

It was on that following Thursday, her mother in law had just left, around 3:30pm, Penny was in enormous pain. I said to her, "Penny, I know your angel is here, please take your angel's hand and go to your Glory." Then I leaned over and kissed her on her right cheek and said, " That's from Nan,"(that's what she called her mother in law), I kissed her on her forehead and said "That's from your son," and then I kissed her left cheek and said, "This is from Me, your friend, Ann." Just then she took her last breath. That kind of scared me but I said " Goodbye, MY Friend, I'll see you soon." She was gone, I had the nurses call her family and the funeral home. I stayed there with her family until they had time to say their goodbyes. Then came the funeral home person. I remember him saying he had no help to take her out. So I said I would help him and asked him what he wanted me to do. I just put my friend in a black body bag and told her that was the last thing I could do! I all but collapsed! That was almost too much but I felt so numb by now that I just had to leave.

You know, when I left the hospital and started driving home, I was in horrible pain from my fibromyalgia, my pain and fatigue was so bad I could hardly breath, it was almost unbearable. It was an affirmation from God as I was thinking, "Oh My God, while I was caring for a friend, I had been totally out of pain and didn't even think about my illness for almost six weeks. God was reminding me what he had done for me as I was helping Penny. To God be the Glory! God has a plan for everyone. We are all born for a purpose in his kingdom. You must open your eyes and listen with your heart and ask him to come in. I tell you the truth, He will come!

I was awakened during the night about one week after Penny's death. It was about 2am when my eyes opened wide. I just jumped up and went to the table and started writing this experience down. I didn't remember a voice or a dream, I just woke up knowing what I was to do. I wrote from 2am until about 6am. WOW, that was powerful!

Now I understand why God had allowed my illness. If I had been working, I would have been unable to fulfill God's plan for Penny and Me, as this is only one of my many testimonies I have had to the Glory of my Lord and Savior, Jesus Christ!

I wonder when His will for me is done in this capacity if my health will be restored or if I just stay in this capacity of helping people? Just a thought, as His will now is all I want for my life!

However, I need to explain a mystery in my life that many of you may have experienced in some way or another. When I was raising my children and working and doing my own thing, everything seemed to be great, but when I heard the voice of God, I knew He is what I wanted and needed in my life. So I started pursuing Him in everyway I could think of. I quit working on Sunday, which paid me double so I gave up a big cut in money, to start going to church. I pursued God in television, I Loved the Sermons that I knew were from the heart and the Bible. My favorite Pastor back then was John Hagee and He still ranks up there. I still try to catch him when I can as I tape His program. He is a great man with unwavering Integrity. I could give him many accolades but right now I feel what he is doing in defense of Israel is his greatest attribute thus far. He spreads his knowledge all over the world, and especially to the White House in hopes that our leaders will take his almighty word from God and quit trying to separate that country, that Will NOT be separated according to God's word! It is so plain in our Holy Bible that God says " Those who Bless Israel, will be blessed, those that curse Israel, will be cursed." I tell you the truth , some of Gods wrath has already taken place and there is lots more to come because of this. Our Great Nation was founded on the Bible, our early leaders governed from the Bible. Our Leaders need to Wake-Up and run to their Bibles!

I love it when I feel the Holy Spirit take over my typing! That is what He wanted said!

In my search for my Almighty God, I started reading the Bible, praying, watching my Christian shows on television nightly, and was going to church, and even got baptized, and was filled with the Holy Spirit. But, I wanted more, the more I knew the more I wanted. I have such a yearning for God, I want to know all His will for my Life! I want to please Him with every breath in my body. When you want more and more from God, even that comes with a price. I had never been attacked by satan until I started pursuing God so hard. Everything and everyone seemed to start attacking me, My life was in chaos. I had found that my dad's siblings had disowned me, because of their greed, my siblings had turned on me. I wasn't understanding what was happening in my own family, It had become a nightmare! It seemed no one wanted to be around me or have anything to do with me. I cried out to God, I asked Him to take me, I had had enough. I didn't know what it was about me that everyone wanted to stay away. I was missing everyone so much and I was truly dumbfounded!

Then, I heard a preacher on television tell me, at least it seemed he was talking to me, that when you are in great pursuit of God, satan will use the people that are the dearest to you to try and tear you away from God. I know it was no accident that I heard that sermon that night. Because, I was at the point that I didn't want to live anymore. Satan almost did me in! Just another thing I had to endure , but now I just hung on to my Savior even harder. I confirmed to satan that he had know place in my life and I would not do anything stupid to glorify him! One night when I went to bed, I was so distraught that I told God I didn't even know what to read in the Bible. I picked it up and ask God to have me turn to whatever He felt I should read. I opened the Bible to Isaiah chapter 43 verse 2 and 3, also verse 10 and 18. This is what my God had for me to read, it was as if He was reading it to Me!" Ann, I have summoned you by name; you are mine. When you pass through the waters, I will be with you; and when you pass through the rivers, they will not sweep over you. When you walk though the fire, you will not be burned; the flames will not set you ablaze. For I am the Lord, your God, the Holy One of Israel, your Savior. You are my witnesses and the servant whom I have chosen. Forget the former things; do not dwell on the past," declares the Lord. What an affirmation from the Lord, in a time when I felt so much despair. With a spontaneous word from God like this, there is no way to continue being down. After reading this, I had No despair left, only total excitement for the Lord, knowing that if I stay true to Him, all would be restored to me that the devil tried to take!

Why would God allow these things to happened, why would He allow satan to enter your world? I have learned that when you are weak, He is strong! He want s to show you that He is always with you, you will never be alone, just as He had told me. He wants you to take everything to Him in prayer. I had always wondered what Ephesians 6 verses 11 through 13 meant. Well, now I can surely tell you. Put on the whole armor of God so that you can take your stand against the devil's schemes. For our struggles are not against mankind but against the powers of the dark world and against the spiritual forces of evil. You see, use God's protection, his armor, so that when the day of evil comes, you can stand your ground! Team God always Wins! But you must be on this team in order to wear his armor!

I remember another night that I was getting into bed and reaching for my Bible, as I sleep so well if I have read the Bible before bed. I have tested this theory, and it proves to be right 100% of the time. I ask God that night to lead me to more conformation that He knows Me and Loves Me, as if he hadn't shown me time and time again. He lead me to another passage in Isaiah Chapter 42 verses 6-9. Most scriptures I would let you read yourself but these love letters from God to me I never get tired of reading! " I, the Lord, have called you in righteousness; I will take hold of your hand. I will

keep you and make you to be a covenant for the people and a light for the Gentiles, to open eyes that are blind, to free captives from prison and to release from the dungeon those who sit in darkness. I am the Lord; that is my name! I will not give my glory to another or my praise to idols. See, the former things have taken place, and new things I declare; before they spring into being I announce them to you." What greater love could I ever need! He is telling me the former heartbreaks are over as I stay faithful to Him, I hang on to Him, I trusted Him, and I Love Him! Now He is sending me out to teach of His Love and truth. No greater joy have I ever known and I will do His will until my death or when He calls me home in the Rapture!

As I continued searching for my redemption, I have asked God so many times to give me a sign of hope to keep me going. On my way to work one day, I was going over Leesburg mountain, in Virginia, I looked up to the clouds for a second and couldn't believe my eyes. I saw the form of a huge Angel and thought How Glorious! Then I slowed down and let the other cars zoom around me, I saw everything about this Angel. The whole face, it was really angelic, the wings extended on the back, the long flowing white gown, the feet, the arms and hands, the long flowing hair and something on the head. But I will never forget that little pointed nose and the features of the face. I tell you, I rubbed my eyes, I blinked numerous times as I couldn't believe what I saw. I was expecting that every time I blinked it would disappear but I saw that Angel for about thirty minutes before it finally left my sight. I thought it would dissipate quickly as a cloud form usually does. I pondered over this for days, trying to realize what I had seen, a mass of clouds that had the form of an Angel, or could I have actually seen a manifestation of a Real Angel! Maybe one day I'll actually meet that Angel and know the truth. I was on cloud nine for a long time after that experience, pardon the pun.

There was another night when I was feeling kinda low and I asked God to give me something to read that would pick me up. He took me once again to Isaiah 41 verse 10-13. " I have chosen you and have not rejected

you. So do not fear, for I am with you; do not be dismayed, for I am your God. I will strengthen you and help you; I will uphold you with my righteous right hand. All who rage against you will surely be ashamed and disgraced; those who oppose you will be as nothing and perish. Though you search for your enemies, you will not find them. Those who rage war against you will be as nothing at all. For I am the Lord, your God, who takes hold of your right hand and says to you, Do not fear; I will help you." I have no idea why God loves me so, but I will continue doing his will for as long as He wants, as there is no greater Love in this world, than HIS Love.

I remember my Grandma, Dads' Mom, wanting to die every time we talked. It use to upset me so much when she would say that. However she was in her 90's then and loved the Lord so much. She finally went to her glory at age 99 ½. I thank God for a Godly Grandma like that, and I finally understand and look forward to the time He has His arms around me in the place He promises all of us when we come to know and Love Him.

About three years ago, I was driving from my son's home in Virginia to my daughter's home in West Virginia, I was driving about forty-five mph, when a deer ran out in front of me and although I tried to miss it, I hit the rear hindquarter. At forty-five mph, even though I had put on the breaks, I hit that deer pretty hard. It was dusk and I couldn't see too much but I heard tons of glass break. It was shattering so hard I could hear it hit the road fiercely. I heard myself screaming as I hit the deer, as it shocked me terribly. I hate hurting any animal and would only hurt something if I had done everything in my power to not harm it. The deer was not killed but ran on through the woods.

I was thinking to myself, as I was looking for a place to pull over, that I have surly tore up the front end of my car! I got out of my car and went to the front to assess the damage and to decide who to call to come get it, as I knew with all the shattered glass I had heard, I had sustained much damage. I couldn't believe my eyes! I walked all around my car and could find Nothing, I mean not one scrape, not one piece of glass, not one dent, only a few deer hair caught in the headlight seam! I continued to drive to my daughter's home and I was totally bewildered! My son-in-law said it was probably internal damage to my lights, even knowing that would not have made the sounds that I heard, he checked them and said their was No damage. He only saw the few little deer hair around the headlight.

After collecting my thoughts, there was only one explanation, God had sent my Angel to protect me! I do believe we all have an Angel to watch over and guide and protect us, But this has been a real conformation as I have never encountered an Angel before. That doesn't mean they haven't protected me before, it just means I hadn't ever noticed before as this I saw and heard with my own eyes and ears!

The Bible says that God will give Angels charge over you and that is just what happened to Me! Thank you, Jesus. Hebrews chapter 1 verse 14 says, Are not all Angels ministering spirits sent to serve those who will inherit salvation? See, this is another blessing that God will give you when you turn your life over to Him! God has given everyone a measure of faith, now is a great time to expand on that faith. Test it and see the wonders your life will have. You see, faith comes by hearing the Word of God and putting it into action in your life, which in turn will bless others around you and will turn others to salvation. You can have no greater blessing than to turn a nonbeliever into a child of God. Taking them from satan's clutches of torment to God's eternal Love!

Many times when I have seen people on the side of the road, holding up their signs for money; hungry, homeless, etc., I will always give to that person as I have such sympathy for them. I was asked one time, what if they are scamming you? My answer was " What if they aren't?" I explained if I give them a little money for food, I have done what my heart said to do and I have no guilt, what they do with the money is out of my hands!

And who knows, Hebrews 13 verse 2 says, Do not forget to entertain strangers, for by so doing some people have entertained Angels without knowing it.

Many times I have thanked God for my illnesses because with them I have been available to be such a big part in the lives of my grandkids. More involved in watching them grow up and being there to interact with them. About three years ago, my youngest grandson, then two, a little guy that started talking at age one had began to stuttering. We thought He was just trying to say words that were way out of his age category, as He was in a great hurry to grow up! When it wasn't going away, we decided to talk to the doctor about our worries. He assured us that he would grow out of it and felt there wasn't anything to worry about. So we didn't pay too much attention to it for a while. After several months, his stuttering became much worse in a short span of time. I noticed he was trying so hard to speak a word that his little eyes rolled back in his head like he was actually loosing his breath trying to get the word out. I was by myself with him and I got so upset that I got sick to my stomach and tears in my eyes. It was the most frightening thing I had ever seen and my heart was totally broken. All I could think of was the awful time he was going to have with this condition, people making fun of him, kids making fun of how he talked and being alienated in school. All these thoughts just rushed in my head and I could not let this happen. I laid him on the floor and put my hands on him and just started praying, "Father, You said in the Bible, ANYTHING we ask in your name, if it's within your will, you will do for those that love you. I beg you to set this baby free of this stuttering and free him of the hell he will face on this earth do to this condition, In Jesus name, amen. I just thanked God for this healing over and over again. This was all I knew to do, I felt so desperate and helpless! After a little while he started to say something. I immediately noticed that he was stuttering a little but was not struggling like before. I immediately started thanking God and praising Him for this miracle. I was so happy, I couldn't hardly wait to tell everyone I knew that God does answer prayer today! I knew the little bit of stuttering he was doing would be ok and he would have a much better life now. I was so pleased that God had heard my prayer, that I was so happy that his stuttering was so much better I just could not thank God enough. That's just what I did all that day. The next day I could hardly believe my ears, my precious little boy had stopped stuttering at all. I had been so happy and satisfied that he was just stuttering a little, praising God for that much, But My Lord and Savior finished the job! I have been thanking Him ever since. I'm telling you, be faithful to Him and He will be faithful to you! 1 John chapter 5 verse 14 and 15. God will test you to see how faithful you are to Him, so in everything be sure to give Him all your praise and glory and thank Him daily for your blessings.

You can just imagine how I felt after being involved in this miracle, I wanted more, and more, and more! " God, This is what I want in my life. Please take me and let me be your servant. I want it all!" I began searching scripture after scripture. I knew in the old testament that Jesus healed the sick, cleansed the leapers, raised the dead, opened blind eyes, and opened deaf ears. But that was Jesus, and I'm just me. As I continued to search, I came upon the day of Pentecost in the upper room of the temple. This was right after Jesus' resurrection from the death on the cross. He told His disciples that He was schools and I took as many of their teachings as I could. I remember something Frances said on one of her teachings. " If Frances and Charles can do this ANYONE CAN! That's what I needed to hear. She was in her 90s and Charles is in his late 80s at this time. I was amazed at the healings I saw on their tapes and also in person. As after taking their courses I went to Texas to be ordained in their ministry. It was a three day wrap up course before ordination. Many lectures, preaching, and I remember Frances hammering this statement " Greater is He that is in me, than he that is in the world. This is referring to the one in us(the Holy Spirit) and the one in the world(satan). What a revelation. 1 John 4 verse 4. The Holy Spirit told me to take someone with me to my ordination. I also knew it would be a long trip by myself as I didn't want to fly and really didn't have the money. So I insisted that my sister go with me and she really resisted, but she came. She was a big grouch the whole way. But it was a 21 hour trip. As we approached our destination she finally calmed down and some of the things she saw was hard to believe. I now know why the Holy Spirit wanted her to be there as if I had just come home and told her about the things I witnessed she would never have believed me. I was having a hard time believing things myself, but I knew I had really come into my belief. Wow! There we were, seeing things happen that we never thought was real, People falling under the Power of God, healings, one after another. People being healed of fibromyalgia, carpal tunnel, legs growing out(due to back problems, one leg being shorter than the other) both problems being healed. Depression being lifted, arms growing out. All of the prayers being healed in the name of Jesus. I was Amazed and in awe of Gods presence in the room. I have never felt anything like that before.

Frances told of a dream that both Her and Charles had almost simultaneously. It was about passing their Mantle(knowledge) on to a younger generation as they

were getting older now. They started their Healing Schools and their schools are now in many countries. I (9remember a story in the Bible about Elijah, a holy man of God, when this man was being called home, he left his Mantle for Elisha and he ask for a double-portion of Elijah's power and he received it. THAT's what I want-A Double Portion! Kings 2 verses 1-14. Elijah never died, he was taken to heaven in a chariot of great wind and fire! And I believe with all my heart, that this is the generation that will be Raptured and never die! We will get into that later.

There were about two hundred people being ordained with me from all around the world. India and

Germany, to name a couple. During our ceremony, we were all called to the front to have hands laid on us for our anointing of Power and Fire. I went up in the crowd and began praying silently to God to anoint me with all He had for me. That I wanted to know it was His anointing and not from just The Hunters. I wanted to be Sure that God was in all of this. As I stood there praying, I felt a little dizzy and my feet started shuffling. I was afraid I had just stood too long with my eyes closed and needed to sit down. JUST THEN, the POWER of God hit me and I flew back at least ten feet. I even hit my head really hard! I laid there in his presents for at least fifteen minutes, not even wanting to be touched or get up. If I had ever felt peace, I knew I was in His Perfect Peace. This was October 11, 2008. He gave me evidence of his power in my hands, as when I got off the floor I felt the palms of my hands tingle. This has never left me to this day!

was alright, what did I feel, did I have a vision, did I hear God's voice, on and on and on. They all wanted to pray with me as they had never witnessed anything like that before, they had all witnessed falling under the power but not ever seeing someone actually coming off their feet and flying back that way. It was just Gods Power, even though I still didn't understand why my head was hit so hard. I just said to them in a joking way, that God was trying to knock some sense into me! After receiving my ordination certificate, and all the paperwork that came with it, My sister and I went back to our hotel room and began packing for our long trip home. I laid down and she put ice to my head and we pondered why I was hit so hard in the head. We didn't have the answers though. So I decided it would just be ok and quit worrying about it. We had a nice trip home and I felt so empowered. A few days later, My head wasn't getting any better, so just to satisfy myself and others, I went to the emergency room and told them I had hit my head. I wasn't about to tell them my story as I knew they would send me straight to the Looney bin! So I signed in and waited for triage. Soon, they called my name. My triage testing was off the charts! What's going on

I thought. So, I went back to my seat and waited for my turn to see a doctor. I got out my Bible and started reading in Romans. It wasn't long before I felt a chill start at my feet and go through my whole body all the way to my head. As this was happening I heard the voice of God say to me "I did not cure what you caused yourself! After I collected myself from that, I went back to triage and told them I was leaving. They said no you need to see a doctor your blood pressure is way too high for you to leave. I told them I would go straight home and take my medicines. I went home kinda laughing at myself as I had such faith that I was healed, that I didn't keep taking my medicines. I said to God, but I have faith, what happened? Just then I realized my head wasn't hurting anymore and I couldn't feel the knot on it anymore! Then it all was revealed to me, if I had not hit my head, and hurt my head, I would not have gone to the emergency room and found out I had not been cured! This sounds unbelievable! The amazing way our God works is awesome. So why didn't God heal me? It sure wasn't my lack of faith! He certainly could have healed me. Maybe He felt this was too easy and I have more lessons to learn on my journey. Maybe I need to be more obedient to His word as I know the things I put in my mouth are detrimental to my health. Maybe by fixing my problems myself I will be able to help more people that have these same issues. Maybe He is determined to make me understand that my body is a temple for the Holy Spirit and should be kept healthy. I think I just got it! I have abused the temple of the Holy Spirit! I got it!

God is always giving me things I type as answers. I just got this right now! God is grieved with the way I don't take care of myself, but will bend over backwards for others! Talk about a revelation, I just got one! Just stay in touch and see how I fix this one! As God is my witness, I will become the temple He wants me to be!

This has just showed me that I, too, must be obedient in ALL things to His Glory! His Word is His Voice! I went to my Bible to look up a scripture for God's temple and there it was, 1 Corinthians 3 verses 16 and 17.The revelations I am having as I write this book are amazing to me. I should not be surprised, as God told me to write this book and I know He is my book reviewer, as many things I am writing just are flowing from my fingers and when I reread some of the things

I have written, I don't remember writing some of it. But to God's Glory, I'll keep going with the flow!

About the time of my ordination, I was visited with another voice, It was much like the voice I heard when God told me to find Penny. He said "Go to the church across the street" then again " Go to the church across the street. I said but Lord, that is a Baptist Church. I need to find a church that believes in Miracles, as I wanted to belong with people that understood my beliefs. I know these churches have Christians in them, but at this point I wasn't looking for Christianity, I was looking for a true relationship with God through Jesus Christ. I was searching for a personal relationship with my Savior. I wanted to hear His voice and interact with Him. I want to evangelize and help fill the Great Commission that we are all called to do. After a couple of weeks of resisting this call, only because I didn't understand what God wanted to use me for. I heard the voice again and told God I would go. I went in and sat down toward the back of the church. I received a few good mornings and smiles and was just setting there waiting for church to begin, when all of a sudden, down the middle isle came a young women, being pushed in a wheelchair by her husband. She had a bandana on her head and her baby boy on her lap with two beautiful little girls following behind. Now I fully understood. I told God I would do His will as now I knew she must need my help! I really am shy by nature, but I took a deep breath, and went up and sat beside her after church. I asked her if there was anything I could do to help her. I think she was totally in shock at my abruptness as she told me later she couldn't believe what I was doing. A stranger wanting to help a stranger.

I explained that I had been sent by God to help her. I knew that would probably scare her but I didn't know any other way to approach her. She thanked me and said she didn't live here that she lived in Berryville, about a half hour away. I told her God knew that as I am in Berryville usually Monday through Friday weekly. As we were talking I noticed she only had one leg, she lost the other to cancer. She told me they had gotten so far behind financially because her husband needed to take her to her treatments and she couldn't find anyone to help with the baby. I said I would take over and help get her husband back to work. She said but you are a stranger, how can got everything on their lists and even more that Christmas, to the Glory of God. I know it is hard to keep a smile all the time when you feel so sick, but sometimes you are not healed as you are in a test of faith. You need to praise and thank God in everything! It hurt me so bad that her attitude had gone from praising God to complaining and smoking as she has Lung cancer. You don't go back to smoking after fighting hard to be cured of lung cancer. I was scared to death to know how God was going to handle this. I was so devastated and felt so betrayed myself. My spirit has been wounded as she began to smoke again. So, I told her I could not help her anymore if she continued to destroy herself with cigarettes as I am allergic to the smell. She has quit again and I am going back to help again! God, Give me strength! She is only thirty-two and her kids need her so much!

Well, back to a happy place. I was driving along the road I live on one day about September of last year, when all of a sudden another deer leaped up toward my windshield, I closed my eyes and screamed. I looked back up and his feet going over me were all but on my windshield, they were not over a quarter of an inch in front of the glass, God had spared me again. My angel must have been dragging him over as I don't have any idea how he missed my car completely, not even a scratch and it looked like to me that his hoofs were pulled up or tucked under some how. I know that God is protecting me for something great. I feel so unworthy of His great love for me and can only hope I will be worthy when I am called! Again, about two months later, I encountered another deer, this time I know my angel was there to protect me. I did what I usually do, I screamed and shut my eyes. When I opened them, I could hardly believe what I saw. The deer's neck was totally looking back over it's back as if someone was pushing that way and it leaped totally backward. That could only have been my angel, with mighty strength pulling that deer's neck backward as I know no neck could bend that way. I was just in awe of what happened. I know one thing though, I have a loving Savior protecting me daily and I praise him daily for his mighty protection. And I know, that I will follow Him to the ends of the earth if that is His will for the rest of my life.

Just this morning, I went to get in my car, the windows were covered with ice and I turned my defrost on. I got back out to scrape my windows and was having a tough time with the ice. It looked as if my defroster wasn't working. Then I realized that my heat was totally gone. It was about twenty degrees out and I started whining. And with seven grandkids I know what whining is! Then I thought, God wants everything in prayer. So I just started praying and thanking God for fixing my heater and got back in my car, and NOT to my surprise, my heater was working! Even as close as I feel to God, I too forget to pray about the little things. I love the verse in the Bible that says "You have not because you ask not! The only way to God is through your prayers in Jesus name!

I have prayed for several people that I don't know, but one of my most blessed times was on the beach in Myrtle Beach, SC. My friend and I were sitting on the beach when we noticed a man and four younger men. We assumed maybe a father and sons. As we approached them to say hi they got real talkative. Two of them, Michael and John were on their way to Afghanistan, one the next day and the other in two weeks. We got to witness to them and they received it so well. I told them, when things get tough, just call on the name of Jesus! It was such a blessing to be able to witness to these great guys as they put themselves in harms way. I continue to pray for them and all our troops and I am asking you to do the same as they fight for our freedom and safety. When I pray for people it seems like I am the one that gets the blessing!

I don't know when Jesus will come back for all his saints, I'm just finding out that I'm one of them. I always thought that when Jesus comes back to earth to rule and reign with His saints, that meant his disciples and the great men of the Bible. But it's Me and You! Pretty cool, don't you think? Jesus will set up His kingdom for ever and ever on this earth. Did you know, that we will live on this earth forever. Most people believe that when we die, we go to Heaven or hell, but Those that love the Lord will spend eternity with Jesus. There will be a New Heaven and a New Earth. When Jesus comes back He will clean up this earth and set up His kingdom and we, those that love God, will rule with Him in the capacity He has chosen for us. The Bible clearly states "World without End." It amazes me of all the hype about the world coming to an end. That the earth will be destroyed and be no more. Where are they getting that trash from. Mine comes straight from the Bible! World without End!

What is the rapture and when will this happen? The Bible says we are not to know the day or hour but we will know the signs and when these signs start we will know that it is soon. There will be wars and rumors of wars, yes there has always been wars, but they will intensify, there will be lovers of money, their money is their God, there will be unnatural relationships, there will be great famines, this is already taking place in many countries, there will be great earthquakes in various places, there has been four that I know of just in the last two months, Haiti, Taiwan, Chile, and Turkey. Brother will betray brother and fathers will betray their children, we can testify to this as we see just how many single mothers we have in this world struggling to care for their children. Children will rebel against their parents. I know I have had the sister and brother betrayal in my own life. I have had uncles and an aunt disown me for greediness. There will be many false christs. I have even heard lately, even people we watch on the daily basis, claiming to be God themselves. That is appalling to me! I tell you the truth, I don't care how much money you have or how many good things you do, you are not Gods and you will not go to your glory but to a fiery furnace waiting in a bottomless pit! New Age, NOT ME, I'll just stick to my Bible that tells me the truth by God's own word! There will be the collapse of our money, leading to the one world order. This is right around the corner! And the gospel will be preached to all nations. This too, is being done through our Christian satellites from several stations and many missionaries putting their lives on the line to go to the nations to tell people the good news of Jesus Christ. God Bless Them All! Mark 13 verses 5-25. But there is good news if you love the Lord, in the next verse, so continue to read Mark 13 verse 26 and 27. And what about the abortions of this generation, murdering precious little souls. Each child killed has a soul, and I know they are in heaven as God has a Huge nursery there. But how about the mothers here, God still loves you but you must repent of these murders and follow Him. These are many of the signs that Jesus' return is soon. We see that the Jews, that were scattered all over the earth are returning to their homeland. As God said his people would return to Israel before the rapture. This is not His coming to earth, this is when He meets us in the clouds, when the dead in Christ will be raised first, that is they will actually come out of their graves, and then those that love Christ will be called up to meet Him in the clouds. Matthew 24 verses 15-35, We will go as we are, our earthly bodies and all, only our earthly bodies will be made imperishable and incorruptible. Can you imagine, NO more cancer, No more arthritis, No more heart disease, No more pain and suffering, No more burying our loved ones or saying goodbye at their bedsides! And all you have to do is call on the name of Jesus and you will be saved. But, don't kid yourself, waiting to call on His name is a dangerous thing as you may be too late. He will come as a thief in the night, at a time that you least expect Him. This is much like the game Russian Roulette if you wait. This is in that last verses I had you to read, about the good news. Read Matthew 24 verse 36-51. Not all people will go, but those that are left, did not welcome Jesus and His teachings. We will cover this in a little while. Stay tuned!

If for no other reason than this, I beg of you to ask Jesus into your heart and live for Him as His way is the only way to heaven and again to earth with life eternal in paradise instead of life eternal in hell! It will be paradise on earth, how great that sounds!

Make no mistake, you can never buy, sell, will, or steal your way into Heaven, Jesus is the ONLY way, it is a free gift of grace, not works, so don't kid yourself! I used to think, and was, a good person all my life just raising my kids and helping people along but had not give my life to Jesus. I really thought this was all that was needed. Wrong Again! Faith without Works is Dead! The Bible says in Revelation 3 verse 15 and 16, Jesus says if you are not cold but not hot, you are only lukewarm and He will spit you out of His kingdom! That was a real eye-opener! That's where I was, living lukewarm. Now understanding what that means, it scared me to Jesus. I've got good news, as you read on farther down that same chapter, verse 20. He tells you He is standing at your heart and knocking. If anyone hears his voice, and will open your heart, He will come in and be with you forever.

If you just repeat the prayer I'm about to give you, but mean it with all your heart, mind, body, and soul, YOU will be Saved!

Dear Father, I admit I'm a sinner, I know you were born of a virgin, died on the cross for my sins and rose again as my Savior, Please come into my heart and save me in Jesus Name, Amen. Just this simple prayer will lead you to salvation. Amazing Grace! I myself have said this prayer hundreds of time! I guess I just wanted to be safe.

I believe my favorite verse(or one of my favorite verses) is John 14 verses 1-4. This is such a comfort to me. Jesus said " Do not let your hearts be troubled. Trust in God; trust also in me. In my Father's house are many rooms, some Bibles say mansions, if it were not so, I would have told you. I am going there to prepare a place for you. And if I go and prepare a place for you, I will come back and take you to be with me that you also may be where I am." Thank you Jesus! All through the Bible are verses like this that just bless my soul.

It's not always easy to be a Christian, When we are cursed, we bless; When we are persecuted, we endure it; When we are slandered, we answer kindly or turn and walk away. There are scoffers, who will try to defeat you as God's Spirit is not in them and they will turn from God's ways. When you encounter them, You must surround yourself in the love of God and pray in the Holy Spirit.

Blessed is the man(or woman) who perseveres under trail, because when he has stood the test, he will receive the crown of life that God has promised to those who love him. James 1 verse 12. I know this verse well, because there were times in my life when I didn't think I could stand anymore and wanted to disappear but this verse helped pull me through one trail, then another would hit me and I would return to this verse to keep me sane!

Are you Rapture Ready? Do you still have fear? We often have fear because of our lack of knowledge. We look at certain parts of the Bible and see God's wrath and put the Bible down because of our fear! I remember when my children were young and I was afraid of everything for them. That dreaded crib death kept me afraid for each of them for the first year, If they had a fever, I was afraid, if they fell, I was afraid, if they went to a friends house, I was afraid, when they started driving, I was afraid, When my son went hunting, I was afraid, when they started dating, I was afraid, When my son's hunting rifle misfired in the house and shattered both front doors, I was afraid, wait a minute, I think I was justified in this fear, as I was in the other room and hadn't seen that he was not hurt. I'll give me that one! If fear could kill you, I would have been dead long ago, but where would I be now? I hadn't given my life to the Lord back then and I shutter to think where I might have ended up!

Jesus says in the Bible, I do not give you a spirit of Fear, only Power. Well now, we know where our fear comes from! I rebuke fear today, it has no place in my life! I look to my Power Source when I have a problem.

The only time you should ever fear, is having the fear of God until you know Him. This is a healthy fear that could ultimately bring you into His kingdom. Knowing Him, there is no fear, without Him there is no Peace! I believe we are in the end times, as I've said before, but I do not fear what's to come as I know my

Savior will protect me and mine. Repent and be baptized in the name of Jesus. I was baptized in the name of The Father, The Son, and the Holy Spirit. I feel I'm coved! As you are baptized you will receive the gift of the Holy Spirit. Acts 2 verse 38 and 39. In the last days, God says, I will pour out my spirit on all people. Your sons and daughters will prophesy, your young men will see visions, your old men will dream dreams.

Acts 2 verse 17-21 and Joel 2 verses 28-32. Also you will read there that EVERYONE who call on the name of the Lord WILL be Saved! That's nothing to fear!

We have a great commission from Jesus himself, He said "Go into all the world and preach the good news of salvation to all the creation." He doesn't say to become a minister, a preacher, or a pastor, He is telling YOU and me to do this. Then he says "Whoever believes and is baptized will be saved, but whoever does not believe will be condemned. And these signs will accompany those who believe : In my name they will cast out demons; they will speak in new tongues; they will pick up snakes with their hands; and when they drink deadly poison , it will not hurt them at all; they will place their hands on sick people, and they will get well". What a gift we have been given to those that believe! Mark 16 verse 15-18. I have tried this and IT WORKS! Not the snake part or the poison, though! As I have no taste for either of these!

In my early years, I had a hard time with believing in things I could not see, I know now I wasn't exercising my faith very well then, but I started looking around for things that were not seen, but I knew were there. Things like air we breath, we sure don't see that, but we sure know it's there, electricity, we see the lights on and our other electrical items on, but we don't actually see the electric currents, so I decided that I could believe in things I couldn't see. Thank God for showing me these things, as I didn't see much evidence of God back then, But He's all over the place in my life now! To God Be The Glory in the things He has revealed to me!

Have you ever wondered why we seem to have just the right amount of workers in the various fields of work. They are evenly distributed throughout our land. I'm talking about in every field there is no abundance in any one of them. Must be a divine plan of God, you think? Make no mistake, God is in control of Everything! He has a divine plan for those that love Him and a divine plan for those that don't! I chose the first divine plan. As God has given us that choice. Choose HIM or choose satan. The choice IS yours!

Now I have come to that dreaded part of the Bible that is so hard to understand for most of us, the book of REVALATION! If you haven't committed your life to Christ, this book should be your final stop before running to Christ. This is a revelation of Jesus Christ. This will explain what will happens on this earth after we are gone so a Christian is to have no fear of this, but if we have unsaved friends and family, this book they need to understand. It's their last chance before the wrath of God on this earth! Remember, Jesus came into this world as a suffering lamb that went to His Slaughter for our sins, He will come back as a Roaring Lion to Set up His Kingdom.

Revelation chapter 1 verse 7 reads, Look, he is coming with the clouds, and every eye will see Him; and all the peoples of the earth will mourn because of Him. So shall it be. Verse 8, I am the Alpha(first) and the Omega(last)," says the Lord God. He then sent warnings to His Churches, and one we have already discussed, If you are neither hot or cold, I am about to spit you out of my mouth. People, it is time to get HOT! In verse 20, Here I am! I stand at the door(heart) and knock. If anyone hears my voice and opens the door, I will come in and eat with him and he with me. See, even in the first part of revelation, Jesus is still calling for us! Now, God's Christians are already with Him in the clouds by the end of the 3rd chapter. What is to come we will only read about now, but have no part in, Thank God!

Revelation 6 verse 1 Jesus opens the 7 seals, The first seal was a white horse, I believe this is satin getting ready to do battle. 2nd Seal opened, a fiery red horse with it's rider given power to take peace from the earth. 3rd Seal opened, a black horse with his rider holding a pair of scales in his hand. This depicts our world economy being destroyed. You will soon be hearing about a one world order, a communist reign, and our money system losing it's value. 4th Seal opened, a pale horse. The riders name is death, and Hades was following close behind. They were given the power to kill one-forth of mankind by sword, starvation, plagues, and the beasts of the earth. 5th Seal opened, the souls of the myrters that were killed for defending God's laws and not taking the mark of the beast. 6th Seal opened, a great earthquake, the sun turned black and the moon turned blood red, the stars in the sky fell to earth. The sky recedes like a scroll, and every mountain and Island is removed from it's place. Every person on earth hides from the face of God. There was no more destruction until God put His seal on 144,000 people of Israel, Jews. Then came the 7th Seal, this seal ushered in the seven Angels who were given the seven trumpets. There was another angel given a censer filled with fire and hurled it on the earth; then came peals of thunder, rumblings, flashes of lightning and an earthquake.

The first angel sounded his trumpet, and there came hail and fire mixed with blood, hurled down upon the earth, a third of the earth, trees, and grass was burned up. The 2nd angel sounded his trumpet, and something like a huge mountain, all ablaze, was thrown into the sea. One-third of the sea turned into blood, a third of the living creatures in the sea died, and a third of the ships were destroyed. The 3rd angel sounded his trumpet, and a great star, blazing like a torch, fell from the sky on a third of the rivers and on springs of water. A third of the waters turned bitter and many people died. The 4th angel blew his trumpet and third of the sun was struck, a third of the moon was struck, and a third of the stars were struck, so that a third of them turned dark. A third of the day was without light and also a Third of the night. The 5th angel sounded his trumpet and a star fell from the sky. This star was given the key to the abyss. When the abyss was opened, locusts came down upon the earth with great power to harm all except those 144,000 that God had set aside. They were not to kill but to torture just the people. The 6th angel sounded his trumpet, then he was told to release the four angels that had been bound at the great river Euphrates. They had been kept ready for this day and time. They were told to kill a third of all mankind. The rest of mankind that had survived these plagues, still did not repent and continued worshiping their demons. The 7th angel sounded his trumpet, and there were loud voices in heaven, which said: The kingdom of the world has become the kingdom of our Lord and of His Christ, and He will reign for ever and ever. Then there was the final wrath of God, the seven bowls of wrath. The first angel poured out from his bowl, ugly and painful sores for the people that had taken the mark of the beast, and worshiped his image. The 2nd angel pored out his bowl on the sea, and it turned into blood and every living thing in the sea died. The 3rd angel poured out his bowl on the rivers and springs of water, and they became blood. The 4th angel poured out his bowl on the sun, and the sun was given power to scorch people with fire. The 5th angel poured out his bowl on the throne of the beast, and his kingdom was plunged into darkness. The 6th angel poured out his bowl on the great Euphrates, and its water was dried up to prepare the way for the kings from the East. Then they gathered the kings to the place called Armageddon. The 7th angel poured his bowl into the air, and out of the temple came a loud voice from the throne, saying, " It is done! Then Jesus comes on His white horse, with His saints(us), to be King of Kings and Lord of Lords! He will reign on this earth for a thousand years, then the final judgment, then He will reign for ever and ever. What a glorious time it will be when He comes back to this earth as He sets up his kingdom and He gives us each our part to do! I have given a taste of what revelation is about, but only a taste, you should now be able to read it and hopefully understand it better. Be sure to read the Good news on Chapter 19-22, which takes you to the end of the Bible! I hope with what I've tried to help you understand, that you will pick up your Bible now and be able to understand the Love our Lord and Savior has for us and the wrath He has planed for those that rebuke Him. I have concentrated mostly on the New Testament as this is the new covenant God made with His people. But make no mistake, the Old Testament has so many prophesy's in it that it is for today.

In the beginning, God created everything! There are great men in the Old Testament. Great stories about the creation of man, godly men like Noah, that built an unthinkable ark to escape the great flood as God was fed up with humanity even back then. He was allowed to save only his family and the animals and beasts of the earth. The Bible tells us, the rapture and wrath of God will occur as people have become like the people of the days of Noah. This is a reference in the New Testament. And Abraham, A man that truly loved God, was tested in the region of Moriah. This is a great story. You will find it in Genesis chapter 22 verses 1-18. The story of Joseph and His brothers. The story of Moses and the Israelites that wondered through the desert for forty years, because of their stubbornness to quit praying to idols. The book of Exodus tells of Moses and the Ten Commandments. This is totally relevant for today. It has great stories of Kings of old, including David, a man that loved God, but he too, made mistakes that God forgave him for. Great stories of Elijah and Elisha in 1 Kings and Elijah taken up to heaven on a chariot of fire and horses. 2 kings chapter 2. The story of the widows oil. I love this story! 2 Kings chapter 4.

The Book of Esther, about a Queen that saved the Israelites, and put her own life at risk. The book of Job, A man that came through so much the devil had done to him, but stayed true to God and was redeemed. This is the book I identified with so much in my hours of need! The Psalms are a beautiful collection of songs and poems that show the love David has for his Lord. Most of us are familiar with Psalm 23. The Lord is my shepherd, I shall not want. He makes me lie down in green pastures, he leads me in paths of righteousness for his name sake. Even though I walk through the valley of the shadow of death, I will fear no evil, for you are with me; your rod and your staff they comfort me. You prepare a table before me in the presence of my enemies. You anoint my head with oil; my cup overflows. Surely goodness and mercy will follow me all the days of my life, and I will dwell in the house of the lord forever. That always touches my heart and does a number on my eyes! Then next comes Proverbs, they are from king Solomon, son of King David. A must read! They tell of the way we should live our lives. You must study Isaiah, as this book is where the passages that God told me to read came from, it will tell you too, of his great love for you. I also love the book of Joel especially Joel chapter 2 verses 28-32. Please read these. These are just a few leading up to the New Testament. No one can tell me that these chapters and verses are not relevant for today. Don't kid yourself! Bless Yourself! Read the Whole Bible! Then go into the world or just your neighborhood and share the good news to everyone you see. We are all to minister to the unbeliever and bring souls into the kingdom. There is nothing you could do greater than THIS!

God Bless You and may Everyone that reads this book come to know Jesus Christ and then follow Him and help with the Great Commission! And please loan your copy of this book to all your friends and family.

In His Service,

Ann

we know it. But for seven years we are being taught the skills we will need when we come to rule and reign with our Savior. Some will be administrators, some will be judges, and most will be teachers, and the Bible will be the Head Book in our schools then! Glory to His Name. You see, there will be many people that will still be alive on the earth after the great tribulation. All over the world Jesus will rule with a rod of Iron, Psalms 2 verse 9. He means business and will make all come to Him. Revelation 19 verse 15. He is right now in Heaven Laughing over this world, as He has everything under control! Psalms 2, verse 4-6. The mountain of the Lord's temple will be established. Read this in Micah 4 verse 1 and 2. The government will be on His shoulders. And He will be called Wonderful Counselor, Mighty God, Everlasting Father, Prince of Peace, from that time on and forever! Isaiah 9 verse 6 and 7. He will judge with righteousness. Isaiah 11 verse 4 and 5. His dominion is an everlasting dominion and will never be destroyed! Daniel 7 verses 13 and 14. If we die with Him, we will also live with Him; if we endure, we will also reign with Him. What greater message of reigning with Him! 2 Timothy verse 11 and 12. Do you not know that we saints will judge the world? Read 1 Corinthians 6 verse 2-4.

Now just visualize these next verses in Isaiah chapter 11 verse 6-9. The wolf will lie down with the lamb, the leopard will lie down with the goat, the calf and the lion and the yearling together; and a little child will lead them. The cow will feed with the bear, their young will lie down together, and the lion will eat straw like the ox.(No more meat eating animals) The infant will play near the cobra, and the young child put his hand into the viper's nest. They will neither harm nor destroy on all my holy mountain, for the earth will be full of the knowledge of the Lord as the waters cover the sea!

Amen.

Notes

Notes

Notes

Notes

_____

_____

_____

_____

_____

_____

_____

_____

_____

_____

_____

_____

_____

_____